PHL

54060000248806

D1556640

*The Fan Museum*

THE
**PAUL HAMLYN
LIBRARY**

WITHDRAWN

DONATED BY

THE PAUL HAMLYN

FOUNDATION

TO THE

BRITISH MUSEUM

opened December 2000

THE
BRITISH
MUSEUM

THE PAUL HAMLYN LIBRARY

WITHDRAWN

391.4409    ALE

Copyright © 2001 The Fan Museum Trust, London

First Published in 2001 in association with The Fan Museum London by
Third Millennium Publishing Limited, a subsidiary of Third Millennium
Information Limited
Shawlands Court, Newchapel Road,
Lingfield, Surrey, RH7 6BL, UK
ww.tmiltd.com

ISBN: 0 9540319 11

All rights reserved

No part of the contents of this book may be reproduced, stored in a
retrieval system, or transmitted in any form or by any means, electronic,
mechanical, photocopying, recording, or otherwise, without the written
permission of The Fan Museum Trust and Third Millennium Publishing
Limited.

All measurements are in centimetres.

Printed and bound in Spain on behalf of Midas Printing (UK) Ltd

# The Fan Museum

Hélène Alexander

The Fan Museum, London in
association with Third Millennium
Publishing, London

*In Memory of Papa and Mama and my Beloved Dicky*

I would Like to thank all those who have helped The Fan Museum over the last decade, the Friends and volunteers without whom the museum could not function, all members of staff and Harley Preston in particular, for keeping us on the 'straight and narrow', the board of Trustees who have given me invaluable support and encouragement, and the photographers Stephen Jackson and Christopher Philips, for the beautiful pictures which 'make' this book

Hélène E Adda Alexander

## The Fan Museum
A modern fairy-tale

It is not often that the result of a lifetime's efforts can provide so much satisfaction and pleasure in the course of that same lifetime!

The Fan Museum stands on its own in more ways than one. First and foremost, it owes its existence to the vision of Hélène and A.V. (Dicky) Alexander, and represents the meeting of minds of these two individuals who founded it, a husband-and-wife team whose love created this unique example of a small independent museum. It is rooted in a long tradition of ancient hospitality inherent in both families. This ethos creates a very special atmosphere both for staff and visitors, redolent of another gentler age, when courtesy and the care of family and extended families were the norm.

Located in two fine town houses dated 1721, which have been lovingly restored internally and externally, the Fan Museum is the only one in the world devoted entirely to the art and craft, the history and geography, in short, to everything pertaining to the fan.

Double potrait of Hélène and Dicky Alexander, by June Mendoza, 1998

When the museum opened its doors to the public ten years ago, in May 1991, the project had already been in hand for some five years. Hélène Alexander is a leading authority on the art and craft of fan-making. During the last thirty years she has amassed a priceless collection – arguably the largest in the country – of fans and related items. And it is this collection that forms the basis of the museum's holdings.

There are more than three thousand objects, including fans, fan leaves dating from the seventeenth century, rare books and fan-related artifacts. The collections are particularly strong on European fans from the eighteenth and nineteenth centuries. Further gifts and bequests have been received since the museum's incipience ten years ago, and contacts have been established with other museums and collectors across the world to ensure that its exhibitions are comprehensive in their coverage of fans.

The museum features two distinct displays. The first is permanent and serves as an introduction to fans: their history, how they are made, the materials used, and the various types and sources of fans. The second, highlighting a particular theme, changes several times each year. The themes – such as children, flowers, animals, birds, religion, and countries with a fan culture – reflect the vast range of subjects that have inspired fan makers through the ages.

Fans are so incredibly varied, they lightly touch the pinnacles of time, they record events, they exude mystery, they can tell us something of their owner, and sometimes they will reveal something of the craftsmen and women who fashioned them. It is hard to think of any one object which can relate so much, and yet fans have, in their lifetime and later, been neglected and often discarded. But it is the infinite variety of the fan which is at the heart of this museum. Not for us to revive a fashion, for fashion is only one aspect of the fan. By its thematic exhibitions the Fan Museum seeks to illustrate in greater depths some areas of life which fans may feature for the more mundane. In this way, for example, religious fans, while showing a biblical subject, will make it more accessible by their small scale, and also by tiny touches such as a little dog, or a loopy-looking not very well-drawn camel, or an exquisite piece of carving of lovers.

The Fan Museum is dedicated to the preservation of fans, as each and every fan holds something of interest: taking a long-term view, even the hideous tourist souvenir fans have a place in this museum, on the assumption that today's 'kitsch' is tomorrow's 'collectable'.

Hélène Alexander, as Director and Keeper, leads a team of experts with unrivalled experience and knowledge, everyone dedicated to the job of displaying, recording and promoting fans. The shop sells high quality fan-related items, many of them unique to the museum, while the old cellars have been transformed into an airy craft workshop for conservation, fan making and training.

The museum is as committed to the future of fan making as it is to the past. One of its aims is to revive the art form by producing contemporary fans, as well as undertaking conservation and restoration. It is a working museum. Lectures and special study courses are held, and the museum's facilities are available for serious research into the subject. The extensive library is available to research students.

It was the wish of the founders of the museum, Dicky and Hélène Alexander, that it should continue to afford pleasure to future generations, and that the level of academic excellence be maintained at all costs, exemplifying their perception of what a museum should be. That the 'old-fashioned' quality of service is kept up may be seen to be anachronistic, but then it may also, in due course, become an integral part of the museum.

If fans and fan making now have a bright future, it is only as a result of years of painstaking preparations and fund raising.

## The Logo and the Trust

In telling the story of the Fan Museum, its elegant logo of a coin backed by two ancient Egyptian-style fans should be explained.

Hélène Alexander was born in Alexandria, Egypt, to a large family many of whom were inveterate collectors. Her father, Victor Adda, was a notable collector and connoisseur of antiquities. He was a numismatist of world renown, and it was his influence which gave his daughter a sense of history and a love of beautiful artifacts. Hélène started to collect fans in the 1950s when an eighteenth-century fan could be bought in junk shops or street markets for as little as two shillings and sixpence. At this time, while still working for a diploma in theatrical design, she was also studying for a degree in history of art. She realized that fans were not only costume accessories with social connotations, they could sometimes be little works of art in their own right. Often they derived from well-known paintings and 'find the source' made an intriguing and endlessly amusing exercise. A passion developed. She was founding president of the Fan Circle International in the 1970s, and had worked for a number of years as volunteer at the Victoria and Albert Museum, where she kept her eyes (and her ears) open, when she made up her mind that some institution should be set up solely for the display and study of fans. Most fans, for reasons of conservation, are kept in the reserves of so many of the larger museums. The idea of small, changing, thematic exhibitions, which would fulfill the criteria required by conservation, meant that fans could at last take their rightful place in the world of decorative arts.

Hélène Alexander resolved to gift her historically important collection to the nation, but it had to be preserved intact, with exhaustive arrangements made for its conservation. It also had to be available for display to as wide a public as possible. None of Britain's established museums could meet those requirements.

The idea of creating the world's first fan museum received encouraging support from Government and leading arts institutions. The Fan Museum Trust was formed in 1984 to administer the museum, with A.V. Alexander as its first Chairman. Trustees were then appointed, charitable status was obtained, and an appeal committee was formed with prominent figures from the arts and business communities.

It was then that a famous coin which had once been in the collection of Hélène's father was presented to the Trust to become its logo. This silver Tetradrachm of Cleopatra VII shows a unique portrait of that legendary queen of Egypt. With Shakespeare's image of Cleopatra in her barge on the Nile fanned by beautiful youths in mind, what could be a more appropriate logo for this tiny, yet in every way exquisite and unique museum?

## The Premises – 12 Crooms Hill

With the help and wise counsel of Hélène's beloved husband, A.V. Alexander, suitable premises for a museum were sought. An early decision was made to locate the museum in Greenwich, an area with a suitably rich cultural heritage. There followed a long and frustrating search for the right setting: a period domestic building was considered appropriate, given the nature and scale of the museum's artifacts. The search ended in December 1985 with the purchase of two Grade II listed town houses dating from 1721. The Victor Adda Foundation played an important role at this point, funding the cost of the buildings as they stood.

And that is when the hard work really began. The houses are outstanding examples of early Georgian architecture, but in 1985 they lay abandoned, virtually derelict. Moreover, the previous owners had carried out crude alterations to the interiors of the buildings, playing havoc with the original architectural features. The location was right and the potential was there, but the Trust now faced the challenge of obtaining planning consent – no mere formality for listed buildings – and raising finance to carry out a meticulous refurbishment and conversion. Some £1.5 million, including the cost of the buildings, was needed for the project.

Work eventually started in September 1987, with Hélène Alexander's late husband, A.V. Alexander, subsequently assuming the role of project management in addition to his chairmanship of the Trust. The refurbishment was to be completed in three stages as and when the funds rolled in from private individuals, businesses, charitable trusts and public bodies.

Nothing was left to chance; the attention to detail was as precise as the craftsmanship on an eighteenth-century fan. The principal architectural features such as the elegant façade, the fine staircase and the beautifully proportioned panelled rooms were retained and restored.

The domestic scale and character of the buildings were further enhanced at the back with a charming reproduction of a Georgian Orangery, the interior painted with murals by Jane Barraclough. It now overlooks a garden that was once a wilderness but has been completely remodelled to include a flagged terrace and – fan-shaped – parterre, with a pool, water cascade and plant groupings in the Japanese style.

The work was completed by the end of 1990. The buildings were restored to their former glory in time for the inaugural exhibition – 'Children in Fans' – in May 1991.

## The Permanent Display

A permanent display on the ground floor forms an introduction to the fan, exhibiting some important dismounted fan leaves of the seventeenth century and unmounted fan leaves of the eighteenth century. One of the early ones features Louis XIV, king of France, with his large family in 1681, and it commemorates the twentieth birthday of his only legitimate son, Louis the Grand Dauphin. This painting recreates, on a small, well-defined surface, an occasion which gives the spectator an insight into another world: life at the court of the Sun King. It illustrates, for those who care to look and are interested enough to observe, that extraordinary orchestrated life led at Versailles and Marly.

Also on the ground floor, the 'Green Room', or orientation room, shows various materials (in their raw state), from which the different components of fans are made. It is thus possible to see in the same case a tusk of ivory and an exquisite and intricately carved ivory *brisé** fan, and a shell of the oriental pearl oyster beside a finely engraved and carved *monture** for a nineteenth-century fan. Here, too, are some of the different materials from which the fan leaf* is made: paper-thin kid skin, vellum, lace, silk, cotton, paper. The display also explains how the materials can be pleated.

The various types of fan are shown, with the clear distinction between the *fixed* and *folding* fan, and the different categories within these types. An amusing section deals with some unusual designs, from a splendid slate fan from Wales (essentially decorative) to *telescopic* fans (which extend on the principle of a telescope), and the 'Swiss Army knife for Corseted ladies', a Victorian fan the guards of which contain little compartments. In these compartments nestle a *vinaigrette\**, a complete sewing kit (with its minute scissors), a mirror and a comb. Finally, the ultimate role of the fan is explored in a display of twentieth-century fans which includes both electrical and industrial ones.

In this room there also hangs a fine double portrait of the founders by June Mendoza.

## The Special Exhibitions

The first floor is devoted to special exhibitions. These are themed exhibits such as 'Flowers on Fans', 'Animal Fans', 'Fans on the Grand Tour', 'A Flutter of Lace', 'Fine Feathers make Fine Fans', 'Advertising Fans', 'Theatrical Fans', 'Art Nouveau Fans', 'Fans of the Four Seasons (Japanese Fans)', 'From Adam and Eve to Fans (Biblical Fans)', 'Fans of the China Trade', and others. Some exhibitions come from other museums where fan holdings are kept in reserve. One such exhibition entitled 'Imperial Fans from the Hermitage' showed a magnificent collection from St Petersburg, never before seen in Europe! Another visiting exhibit from the Peterhof Palace included garments, purses, intimate mementos, in fact 'Personal Treasures of the Tsars', as well as the fans themselves. 'Unfolding Beauty – a secret collection' featured the fine collection belonging to the Worshipful Company of Fan Makers.

The exhibitions last for a maximum of four months, since, for conservation reasons, it is not advisable to leave folding fans (in particular) open for a longer length of time. The museum is indeed very conscious of the delicate nature of fans and of the careless ways they have been treated in the past. Levels of light and humidity are carefully controlled, all windows are furnished with UV filters, and lighting in the cases is fibre-optics (a cold lighting which will not cause warping).

One of this year's exhibitions celebrates ten years of the Fan Museum with a display of its masterpieces. Perhaps the most valuable object in the collection is a fan leaf, not usually on view, by PAUL GAUGUIN, painted in 1887 when he was in Martinique. This unpretentious, delightful design for a fan takes pride of place beside a fully made-up fan dated 1882, painted by CESARE DELL'ACQUA, and given to Princess Stephanie of the Belgians by her aunt and uncle on the occasion of her wedding to the Austrian Emperor Franz Joseph's only son. Painted at approximately the same time, two more different works of art can hardly be imagined! 'Stephanie's fan' with its gold guards encrusted with a design made up of over 1500 tiny diamonds, its leaf well painted on both sides with a pastiche costume piece, by an artist at the peak of his popularity (indeed a success in his own time), contrasts with Gauguin's light-suffused view of a hut in a verdant rolling landscape with a pale blue sky overhead and a feeling of peace and tranquillity.

If the recipient of the gold fan with its fine painting is known – indeed, she and her story are now history – what of another masterpiece shaped like a double-barrelled flintlock gun, fashioned from ivory, each stick carved so finely as to resemble lace? For whom was this fan made?

## The Study Room

In addition to the exhibition areas, the study room is also located on the first floor. This beautiful, quiet place is seldom seen by the public though it is perhaps the 'engine room', the real heart, as it were, of the musuem. Lined with purpose-built rows of drawers and bookcases of walnut veneer banded with a tiny fillet of silver, this area houses the reserves, fans which are not on show, archival material, books and dictionaries, all the materials necessary to academic study of fans – those small objects which are a microcosm of the World. In this chamber with its furniture made to specification by master craftsman Robin Williams (a pupil of the celebrated John Makepiece), students may come and study under the supervision of experts; material is sifted; exhibitions are planned and recorded; and fans are brought in for identification or for conservation to be carried out by a fully trained specialized conservator.

This serene room is also used for meetings of the Trustees of the Fan Museum, a body responsible for the running of a self-contained yet spreading small enterprise. In fact, it could be said that the museum operates like a folding fan, the board of Trustees being the rivet\*, the heart of the articulation of the fan as it opens up!

## A Brief History of Fans

Few art forms combine functional, ceremonial and decorative uses as elegantly as the fan. Fewer still can match such diversity with a history stretching back 4,000 years.

Fans have been used as advertising giveaways; they have been vital fashion accessories to the high society ladies of the eighteenth century; at the time of the Pharaohs they were used for ceremonial purposes and had religious and magical connotations.

Fans continue to command attention, only now they are coveted as collectable items.

The earliest fan remains were discovered in Egyptian tombs, the most famous being the Tutankhamun fan with its L-shaped ivory handle, still complete with ostrich feathers.

Even then, fans came in all sizes and served both practical and ceremonial purposes. They were sophisticated – and elegant – objects: their wooden handles were typically covered in gold leaf, decorated and enamelled, and they held colourful feathers or woven slats.

There is evidence that the Etruscans and the Greeks had fans at an early date. Chinese literary sources, meanwhile, associate the fan with ancient mythical and historical characters, and such is the advanced state of fan development in China that intricate painted silk fans existed as far back as the fifth century. Eastern influences were important to the development of fans in Europe.

A form of folding fan first appeared in Italy about 1500. Up to that point, fans had typically consisted of a stick with a fixed flat rectangle of vellum, paper or stiffened material which was painted, woven, embroidered or sometimes embellished with tassels and fringes. There were also fixed feather fans with handles fashioned from a variety of materials.

## 1. Landscape in the Martinique

Of the three great masters of Post Impressionism – Cézanne, Van Gogh and Gauguin – only Gauguin painted fan leaves intended as gifts and certainly inspired by many fan paintings of the 'father figure' of the Impressionist and Post Impressionist artists, Camille Pissaro (1830–1903). Gauguin frequently quoted motifs from his easel paintings on his fan leaves from various periods, and 24 leaves are recorded as well as several preliminary sketches and prints and one fan-shaped oil painting. The present example, seemingly the only one known to be in the United Kingdom, dates from 1887, just after his Martinique visit. Others survive from his residence in Tahiti where his lifelong striving for a form of personal stylistic 'primitivism' reached a final climax.
Signed and Dated GAUGUIN* 1887.
Depth of leaf 12 cm

*GAUGUIN (Paul) 1848–1903.
Lit: Jean Pierre Zingg. *Les Éventails de Pâul Gauguin*, Paris (1996), pp. 38, 88, pl. XI.
Provenance: Paco Durrio, Paris; W. Geiser, Bale 1936
LD Fan 2000.1. Anonymous gift in memory of A.V. Alexander CBE, first Chairman of The Fan Museum Trust

## 2. Avec Privilege du Roy

An unmounted printed fan leaf with a central cartouche surrounded by garlands of fruit and baroque motifs upheld by four *putti*. Within the oval is a *masque* representation of 'the Judgement of Paris'. Two circular framed *vignettes* contain representations of Eros, the whole leaf being designed with a wide baroque border with leaves, fruit and more *putti*. Beneath the central vignette is a cartouche inscribed *Faict par* BOSSE* *avec Privilege du Roy pour cinq ans 1636*
Total span 54 cm
French c.1636

*BOSSE Abraham (1602–1676). Essentially an engraver, Abraham Bosse is known to have engraved at least two series of fan leaves and some leaves for fixed fans. In an engraving entitled *La Galerie du Palais* dated 1635, Bosse recreates a scene of polite society of the time. Wealthy Parisians saunter by boutiques selecting from the books, gloves, collars, lace and fans on offer. A shopkeeper turns to the shelves to lift down a box clearly inscribed *Eventails de Bosse* (fans by Bosse) – showing that the artist was not beyond a bit of self-advertisement.
Lit: Hélène Alexander. *Fans*, London, 1984.
Hélène Alexander Collection FL17

### 3. The Grand Dauphin's 20th Birthday

Extended fan leaf (not pleated or mounted up).
The scene painted in gouache on vellum shows Louis XIV of France, the 'Sun King' seated beside his queen, Marie Thérèse of Austria. Beside the king stands their son Louis (Le Grand Dauphin) in blue and silver (the colours of Royal France). A female figure representing France in a cloak of blue scattered with silver *fleur de lys* kneels before him and, assisted by *putti*, empties a cornucopia of gold coins at his feet. There are eleven other figures on either side of the royal couple and three more stand behind the thrones. Some of the figures in the royal circle have been identified. To the left of the Queen are Philippe duc d'Orléans, brother of the King and his wife Elizabeth Charlotte (Liselotte) von der Pfalz, then 'La Grande Mademoiselle', the king's first cousin and others. To the right of the king, after his son, come the Dauphin's wife and seven others. Three gentlemen with their backs to the viewer indicate that these are members of the French royal family deceased in that year.
Length 43 cm x 27.5 cm
French c.1681

Lit: *Liselotte von der Pfalz.* Heidelberg, 1996
Purchased for The Fan Museum with an anonymous gift matched by a donation from the National Arts Collection Fund
LD Fan 1997.35

### The Sun King

Louis XIV of France took a personal interest in everything that went on in his kingdom, and he was particularly interested in arts and manufacture, much encouraged by his minister Colbert.

A project for a fan leaf is known, with annotations in the king's hand for alterations and additions. It seems that Louis was even interested in fans!

## 4. *Monsieur*

An extended fan leaf relating to the siege of St. Omer, at which 'Monsieur',
PHILIPPE duc d'Orléans*, younger brother of Louis XIV, can be seen on a prancing horse
in his role of general in the course of this campaign (1678).
Period frame of carved gilt wood.
Length 47 cm x 24 cm
France c.1678

*PHILIPPE, duc d'Orléans (1640–1701).
Lit: Pamela Cowan, 'Les Éventails s'ouvrent pour Louis XIV', in *Fans* (Bulletin of the Fan
Circle International, Winter 2001, issue 72).
Hélène Alexander Collection

## 5. *La Campagne de Flandre*

An extended fan leaf on which the French army in battle order can be seen before a
Northern city fortified *à la Vauban* where some of the buildings are already in flames.
Cannon placed in half-circle batteries are firing on the assailants.
(The fan leaf has been removed from the monture, extended and stuck to a wooden
backing.)
The figure in the *gorge* is an addition which dates from the time when the fan was dis-
mounted. It is that of a general and probably refers to the death of TURENNE*, one of
Louis XIV's generals who was killed by a stray bullet near the town of Sasbach.
Period frame of carved and gilt wood.
24 cm x 42.5 cm
French c.1690

*TURENNE (Henri) de la Tour d'Auvergne, Vicomte, Maréchal de France (1611–1675)
Hélène Alexander Collection

## 6. Bacchus and Ariadne

'Chicken skin' fan leaf, painted on both sides. The main face is painted with a magnificent copy of GUIDO RENI's painting of Bacchus and Ariadne. Ariadne abandoned by Theseus, her hair undone and blowing in the sea breeze is surprised by the god of wine, seen here as a handsome young man with his train of *bacchante* and numerous *putti*. The reverse, with Eros sailing a tiny craft beyond which are hills and a temple, is framed by garlands of vines and luscious grapes.
Total span 51 cm
Italy c.1750

*RENI Guido (1575–1642) Painter whose work owes much to the Carracci of whom he was a pupil, to Raphael, Correggio and the Cavaliere d'Arpino. His elegant style revived his popularity in the 18th century when visitors on the 'Grand Tour' were able to admire his many works. Indeed he was known as 'the divine Reni'. His *Bacchus and Ariadne* was in the collection of King Charles I of England. When Queen Henrietta Maria was in need of funds she sold the painting to an Italian banker. At his death his widow had the painting destroyed, deeming it to be too lascivious. It was then only known from contemporary engravings.
Hélène Alexander Collection FL16

## 7. Gunbai Uchiwa

A fixed iron fan; the shaped metal 'frame' holds a lacquered screen upon which a reddish-golden dragon curls itself around the handle of the fan which bisects the screen. Shaped metal plaques finely engraved with a flower and leaf design are riveted to the screen on all sides. The handle, also riveted to the frame, is partly encased in shaped and engraved metal casings. On both sides of the frame where the screen and handle meet are two tiny gold metal fans in relief. The lower section of the handle has an ornamental ferrule, but the cord once threaded through is now lacking.

Total length 59 cm
Edo Period: 18th century
Hélène Alexander Collection 1617

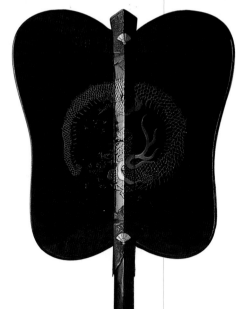

## 8. The Meiji Court

Court fan *(hiōgi)* in *hinoki* (cypress) wood, painted on both sides. On the obverse are painted 'the three friends', the pine tree, blossoming plum and bamboo, flanked by two flying cranes and golden clouds with a tortoise emerging from the grass at the base. The reverse shows a design of butterflies with gold and silver clouds. From each guard hang six long plaited silk cords (which are supposed to represent the six virtues) in green, yellow, dark brown, orange, pink and white (approximately 1.5 metres in length). The metal rivet is capped with a metal butterfly on one side and a metal bird on the other.

Length 36.5 cm
Meiji Period: c.1880
Hélène Alexander Collection 1466

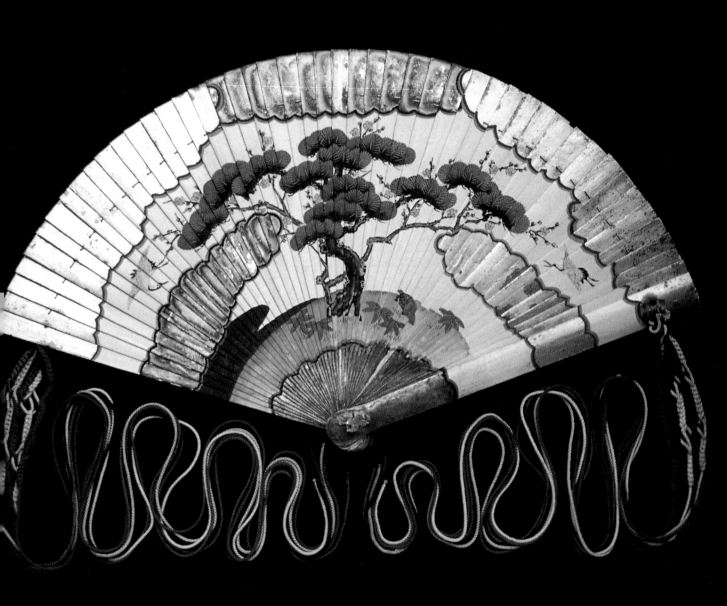

## 9. The Waterfall of Wisteria

Ivory *brisé* fan, the guards decorated on both sides with fine *Shibayama* work; on one guard is a trellis of wisteria in full bloom, on the other are three leafy bamboo shoots with a flying crane above. When open the fan reveals an obverse showing an extensive landscape beneath a silver moon, a traveller of substance with his accompanying servant welcomed by another man to his abode beyond a bamboo stockade. The reverse is also decorated in gold *hiramaki-e* and *takamaki-e* with fruit and convolvulus. The white metal loop is furnished with an 'important' double silk tassel. Fans of this quality were often made as presentation pieces to Europeans and Americans and for the top overseas markets.

Length 23.5 cm
Edo Period: 1860's
Hélène Alexander Collection 1580

Detail of right hand guard

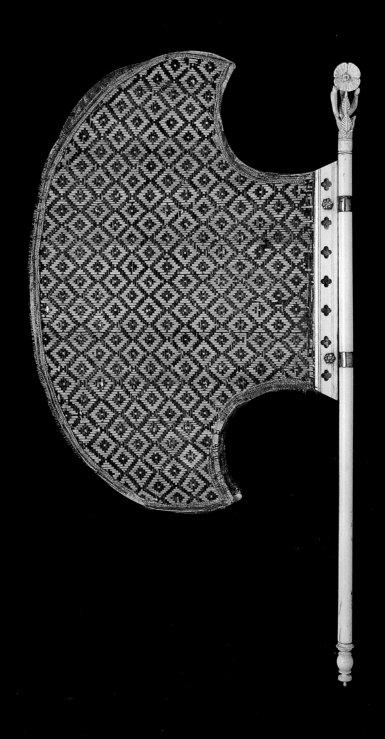

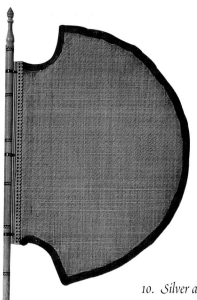

## 11. Mughal Elegance

Axe-shaped semi-fixed fan with a fine ivory handle with decorative incised bands and elegant finials at top and bottom. The leaf is suspended from the handle by three silver rings fixed to two slats of crenellated ivory, thus making it capable of being swung around. It is made of paper-thin strips of ivory woven to form an axe-shaped surface bound in saffron yellow silk.
Length to handle 34.5 cm

Mughal (India) late 18th century
The Mughals established their empire in India in the sixteenth century, and it achieved its highest peak under the dominance of Aurangzeb (1659–1707), after which it declined, allowing infiltration by European powers, France, England and Holland in particular.
Hélène Alexander Collection 608

## 10. Silver and Ivory

Axe-shaped semi-fixed fan with ivory handle and finials, one with a flower which is probably a replacement. The double leaf is suspended from the handle by two silver bands fixed to two ivory slats which are pierced with floret shapes which were probably once filled with precious stones. The two stays hold the double leaf together with double headed silver nails. Both leaves which are held together as described are made from paper-thin woven strips of ivory and silver 'ribbon', each one forming a different pattern. The outside of each one is bound, first with paper (some of which has become visible) over which is stitched a silver cloth binding.
Length of handle 37 cm

Mughal (India) late 18th century
Lit: Two metallic thread and woven ivory fans are illustrated in *Fans from the East*, London, 1978.
Hélène Alexander Collection 788

## 12. From the Imperial Workshops'

A fixed fan, mainly of cinnabar lacquer, the obverse intricately carved
with tiny figures in an elaborate landscape. The reverse is black lacquer
with an applied carved stone flower and dog (possibly applied at a later
date). There seems to be little doubt that owing to the high quality of the
work this ceremonial fan was made in the imperial workshops which
were set up in the Forbidden City in Beijing under the Emperor Kangxi
(reigned 1662–1722). The fan probably dates from the reign of the
Emperor Qianlong (1736–1795). This is a period which is well-known for
the production of very fine carved lacquer, mainly red cinnabar. It is
recorded that the Emperor had a particular fondness for this material and
commissioned many pieces from the imperial workshops, including large
hanging panels depicting his battle glories! (Ben Janssens, Oriental Art Ltd).
Length 45 cm
Chinese, Qing Dynasty, 18th century
Provenance: formerly in the Mitsui family collection, Japan.
Hélène Alexander Collection

Below: Detail

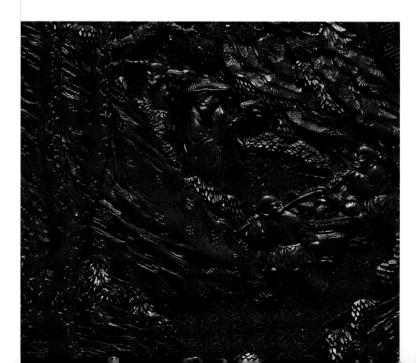

### 13. *Mythical Beasts*

Ivory and mica fan, the guards painted in reds and greeny-greys, with pierced sticks and a painted paper leaf with mica insets forming shapes which are painted in to form animal creatures from Chinese mythology. The *head* of the fan, shaped as an inverted tulip, and the dome-shaped rivet are characteristic of some early export fans.
Length 26.5 cm
Probably Macao c.1690
Hélène Alexander Collection 324

Below: The same Fan seen against the light

## 14. The Wheel of Love

Ivory fan, the sticks pierced, the guardsticks painted in red in the *Imari* style. The head of the fan (i.e. the lower end) is shaped as an inverted tulip. The leaf is painted in red with a large oval panel of mica painted on both sides (mirror image) with figures of a curious looking couple and another man; in the centre beneath some drapes a wheel is carried by two very pink winged elves meant to represent cherubs. The figures are quite clearly painted by an oriental wishing to represent Westerners. The metal dome-shaped rivet and the 'inverted tulip' pattern indicate an early export fan, probably made for the Portuguese, with Japanese influence in the guards.
Length 25 cm
Probably Macao c.1680
Hélène Alexander Collection 1247

## 15. The Hongs at Canton

Ivory *brisé* fan, the guards deeply carved with lotus
motifs. The sticks are carved, pierced and pared to reveal
the HONGS at Canton* in the late 18th century, each with
its national flag. Large and small craft can be seen in the
river beyond them.
Length 29.5 cm
Made in Canton for the European or American trade
c.1785

*The HONGS at Canton were not only the residences but
also the trading headquarters for Western merchants.
Each country engaged in the trade occupied a hong which
consisted of a front building facing the Pearl River and a
series of other buildings behind connected by courtyards.
Each building contained public rooms and dining facilities
as well as rooms on the upper floors. Each hong is recog-
nisable behind its respective flag, but there were changes
between 1760 and 1856 with hongs moving to different
powers. America did not enter the China Trade until 1785.
Hélène Alexander Collection 680

### 16. The Gun

A rare ivory *brisé* fan in the form of a double-barrelled flintlock gun, the sticks pierced and the guardsticks silvered and applied with gold at the top (one plaque missing) and carved to form the barrels, trigger and lock-plate. Probably Dieppe carving.
Length 29.5 cm
French, late 1780's

A firearms expert states that this is a replica of a French gun of the 1780's. Another fan along the same lines as this one is known in a private collection, but is made of wood applied with a central print showing Lafayette reviewing his troops.
Hélène Alexander Collection 332

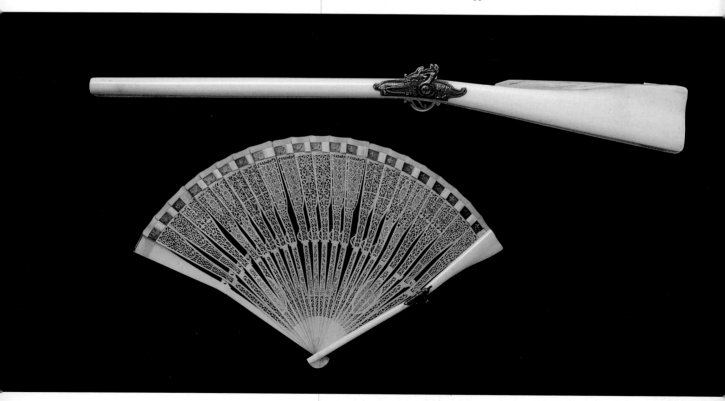

## 17. *Please*

Ivory *brisé* fan, carved, pierced and painted with a central *vignette* of a lover kneeling beside a somewhat dishevelled lady in
a rose garden, a winged *putto* with an
arrow flying off towards a statue of Eros.
The reserves are pierced, silvered and
painted with simulated 'jasperware'
plaques and an elegant lady on one side
and a *beau* on the other.
Length 27 cm
c.1790's
Provenance: Gorand Hurtès collection
Hélène Alexander Collection 1550

## 18. *For Chaste Diana*

Ivory *brisé* fan with finely pierced sticks
and guards, silvered and gilded in three
tones of gold and painted. In the centre
are two ladies in classical dress, one seated
in a chariot drawn by a pair of prancing
horses. In the reserves are two medallions
painted with a hunter in green classical
dress holding an arrow and leading a dog
on a lead in one of the ovals, and in the
other Diana, in a pink tunic holding a bow
and arrow reaching for her quiver.
Curiously amatory motifs abound, a rose
alternates with flaming hearts, doves with
a letter and a ring, and musical instruments.
Concealed pivot.
Length 21.5 cm
Probably French c.1790's
Hélène Alexander Collection 1587

## 19. Double Entente

Ivory fan with serpentine sticks, the guards painted in gold with a design of birds painted in gold on branches of flowering shrubs. The scalloped 'petals' are made of painted silk with two gold and two silver faces.
On the gold background; On the left is a sleeping figure on a dais; a woman on his left is pointing him out to Love who rides behind Venus' chariot. In the foreground is Venus on her chariot drawn by two *amorini*. On the right a woman seated on a dais claps her hands while a young man plays an air on a trumpet. A frieze of parrots and dragonflies borders the picture.

Roses in full bloom and rose buds form garlands on a silver background. On the other gold background there are three 'scenes' of a somewhat exotic nature. To the left is a character wearing a long blue and pink robe and sporting a headdress of feathers: beside him another feeds a bird. In the centre another personage is seated beneath a canopy. On the right is a man in a short tunic with blue sleeves wearing a feathered cap.

On the next silver background are garlands of blue flowers and quince with dragonflies and butterflies.
Although the theme of this fan is Love, there are strong exotic elements which tie in with the taste in the 17th century for so-called 'Indian' décor where Chinese and other countries are mixed up. They stem from the lovely objects which were arriving in France, Holland and England via the great East India Companies.

The visit of ambassadors to the Court of Louis XIV in particular resulted in exotic ballets and in the making of many objects with motifs deriving from these far away places which a craftsman would only know from prints or a glimpse of one of the strange birds or beasts kept by the aristocracy. Parrots were prominent among these creatures.
Length 19 cm
Possibly French c.1670
Hélène Alexander Collection 1620

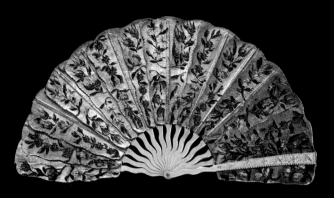
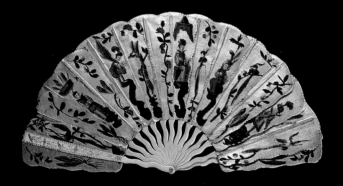

20. *Marie Leszczynska's Wedding*

Folding fan with blond tortoiseshell *monture*, piqué'd in gold with *fleur de lys*, scrolling foliage and flowers. The guard sticks are embellished with the Arms of France quartered with those of the KING OF POLAND*. The double 'chicken skin' leaf is painted on both sides. On the obverse is an allegory of marriage with a couple in classical attire crowned by Hymen with nymphs and *putti* on the right crowning France's blue shield with its three *fleur de lys* and that of Poland with its red band and three white eagles. The reverse is painted with Minerva and Cupid in conversation.
Length 28 cm
French 1725

*KING OF POLAND: Stanislas Leszczynski (1677–1769).
Louis XIV of France was succeeded in 1715 by his great grandson Louis XV (1710–1774) and France was governed by a Regency until 1725 when Louis XV was married, at the tender age of 15, to Marie, daughter of the King of Poland, Stanislas Leszczynski. She was several years older than her little husband.
Hélène Alexander Collection 1574

*21. The Marriage of Louise Elizabeth of France*

Sticks carved, pierced, painted and applied with mother-of-pearl rococo motifs with musicians, putti and wildlife, the guards similarly decorated. The double paper leaf painted in the body colour on the obverse with two ladies (one a French Princess) at a harbour shore, receiving the Spanish Ambassador and another gentleman, beneath a cartouche inscribed *Le Feu de Monsieur l'Ambassadeu* and showing a fireworks display at Versailles, flanked by a castle (Castille) and a blue shield with three *fleur de lys* (the arms of France). In the reserves are two vignettes surmounted respectively by a lion (Leon) and a cockerel (France) and inscribed *Le Temple de la Paix* and *Le Feu du pont Neuf.* The reverse with figures in a landscape and two men in combat from boats.

Length of guard 29 cm

French c.1739

Commemorative of the marriage by proxy of Louise Elizabeth of France

(1727–1759), eldest daughter of Louis XV of France and Marie Leszczynska. In 1739 she was married to the Infante Don Felipe (1720–1765), later Duke of Palma, Piacenza and Guastalla, younger son of Philip V of Spain. The marriage was conducted by proxy at Versailles on 26 August 1739, and then in person at Alcala de Henares near Madrid on 25 October of the same year. Celebrations in France were marked by a firework display at Versailles and in Paris.

The ladies painted on this fan wear French dress of the period, the men wear the distinctive style of the Spanish Court.

Hélène Alexander Collection 643

22. *The Birds*

Ivory *brisé* fan painted on both sides. On the obverse within a border is a well-painted assortment of birds with peacocks, parrots, turkeys and other birds among buildings and trees painted *en camaïeu*. The birds are in the manner of HONDE-COETER\*. The *gorge* is painted with *chinoiseries* as are the guards, both on the inside and the outside. The reverse is a landscape *en camaïeu* blue, the figures of the peasants standing out in colour. In the *gorge* are six blue and white Chinese export vases.
Length 21.3 cm
Dutch c.1700
Lit: F. de Perthius and V. Meylan, *Éventails*, Paris 1989, ill. p.33.

\*HONDECOETER, Melchoir de (1636–1695). Dutch School – painter of exotic birds and engraver – sometimes called 'the Raphael of birds'!
Hélène Alexander Collection 1435

## 23. Timepiece

An ivory folding fan, the sticks and guards carved and
pierced and painted *en grisaille* and gold. The carved-
flower-shaped pivot is inset with a landscape miniature
and a watch said to be by John Thierry of London (in
working order). The fine kid leaf is mounted *à l'anglaise*,
the obverse painted with an allegorical scene of a warrior
kneeling before a princess at the altar of Love with an
attendant Hymen bearing a torch and two winged cherubs
in the foreground. The reverse is painted with a romantic
landscape.
Length 26.5 cm
Probably English c.1750's.
Said to have belonged to Queen Victoria's mother, the
Duchess of Kent.
Hélène Alexander Collection 500

## Ruth

Ruth, a Moabite woman, followed her mother-in-law Naomi, to Bethlehem after the death of her husband. She was allowed to glean in the fields belonging to Boaz, a wealthy kinsman of Naomi. In due course Boaz married Ruth who bore him a son, the grandfather of David. Thus Ruth, by traditional reckoning was an ancestor of Christ.

44

### 24. Ruth and Boaz
Ruth 2:16–17

Mother-of-pearl fan, with delicately carved and pierced sticks, the guards carved with vases of flowers, figures and dolphins. The tops of the sticks are *palmette* shaped. The fine single vellum leaf is mounted *à l'anglaise* and is painted both sides. On the obverse, the figures of Ruth and Boaz occupy the centre of the leaf, while men and women work in the field, cutting and binding sheafs of corn and loading hay onto a cart, while a dog (symbol of fidelity) sits beside a resting group. The reverse is painted with an ox-drawn cart being loaded with hay within a delicate exotic border. Good paste rivet.
Length 25.7 cm
c. 1720–30
Hélène Alexander Collection 1199

### 25. Ruth
Ruth 2:16–17

Ivory fan with carved, pierced, silvered sticks and guards, featuring a pair of lovers in a pastoral setting, elaborate scrolls and cornucopia. The vellum leaf, mounted *à l'anglaise*, is painted *en grisaille* on both sides. On the obverse a fine composition of a harvest scene is revealed within a border with cleverly designed *repoussoir* figures of Boaz and Naomi in the reserves. Ruth can be distinguished in the foreground of the harvest scene, gleaning. RUTHA SPICAS LEGIT POST MESSORES is inscribed beneath the figure of Naomi. On the reverse a young woman with a winnowing basket amid thorn bushes and a *chinoiserie* design are painted *en grisaille*.
Length 29 cm

c. 1750–60
Hélène Alexander
Collection 784

## 26. The Mask Fan

Bone fan, the sticks painted with flowers, the guards carved with baroque scrolls. The paper leaf is a hand coloured etching, the centre part being a face, extending into the *gorge* and with cut out eyes, forming a mask. The four *vignettes* on either side show, from left to right, a music shop, two scenes from the theatre, the right one showing a London street, and a fan shop in which mask fans are on display, one being offered to a lady in a yellow dress.
Length 26.5cm
English c. 1740's

N.B. These fans are very rare. There are only some seven printed ones known, and a handful of painted mask fans, the most noteworthy one being in the collection of the Hermitage Museum, St. Petersburg.
Provenance: The Baldwin Collection
Hélène Alexander Collection 151

Esther 2:17
'..and the king loved Esther above all women, and she obtained grace and favour in his sight more than all the virgins; so that he set the royal crown upon her head and made her queen instead of Vashti…'

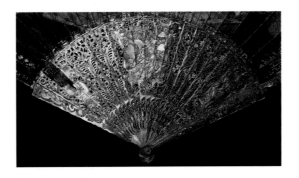

## 27. The Crowning of Esther

Mother-of-pearl fan, the sticks and guards elaborately carved and gilt, the sticks being further backed with *burgeau* or 'goldfish'. The double leaf is painted on both sides. On the obverse, within an elegant border is a well-painted scene with a lady in 'eastern' attire being crowned while a crowned and turbaned king in a very French *fauteuil* looks on. On the left in the reserve outside the picture, as it were, sits a man with a long pipe (possibly Mordecai).
Length 30 cm
French Court fan c. 1750–60

N.B. The face of Esther is not unlike that of Mme de Pompadour in the two paintings of her in Eastern dress by Carl van Loo, which her brother said were the only portraits to give a true likeness of the Marquise.
Hélène Alexander Collection 1202

50

### 28. *Ranelagh Gardens*

Ivory fan, the sticks and guards carved and pierced with
vases of flowers gilt and painted in the Chinese manner
with blue ribbons and blossom simulating blue and white
china. The leaf is painted with a view of Ranelagh Pleasure
Gardens showing the famous Rotunda, with a 'Chinese'
pavilion in the foreground and figures. The subject is after
a lost painting by Canaletto. The single leaf, mounted *à
l'anglaise* is painted on the reverse with *chinoiserie* figures
and flowers.
Length 26.5 cm
English c. 1755
Hélène Alexander Collection 1000

## 29. Esher House

An important topographical fan: ivory with sticks and guards pierced painted and gilt, with *putti* in the guards and flowers on the sticks. The vellum leaf is painted with a fine house in the 'Gothick' style by a river with figures on both banks. A craft with the 1707 Union flag and the flag of St. George is coming to land with elegant passengers aboard. The house has been identified as Esher House Surrey, home of the Pelham Family, taken from a print dated 1758. The fan is mounted *à l'anglaise*. The reverse is painted with a single figure in the centre with flowers and blue and white porcelain at the sides.

Length 26.5 cm
English c. 1759
Hélène Alexander Collection 1590

51

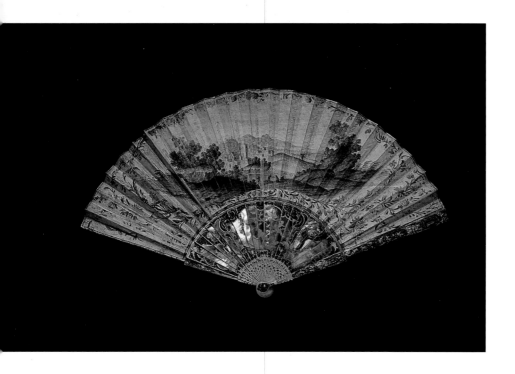

*30. The Architect*

Ivory folding fan with intricately carved, pierced, painted and gilt sticks which are backed with 'goldfish' and feature gilt shepherds and shepherdesses and rollicking *putti* on a background of rococo curves and shapes. The double *'chicken skin'* leaf is painted on both sides, on the obverse with a scene in a garden with scaffolding and building work in progress. In the centre of the picture a couple with an *abbé* discuss plans which the architect is pointing out to them with his dividers while another smart couple look on with interest. Workmen with ladders busy themselves in the background. On the left reserve is a somewhat incongruous painting of a goat, a large marrow growing beside it and a lad in red looking on. The reverse is painted with an extensive landscape with buildings (restoration on the reverse and replacement rivet).
Length 29 cm
c. 1750
Hélène Alexander Collection 1616

### 31. The Birth of the Dauphin

Commemorative fan for the birth of the Dauphin Louis Joseph (1781–1789).
14 sticks pierced, carved, gilt and painted with dolphins, the arms of France, and in the centre a baby in a cradle and a nurse, the guards both articulated and backed with mother-of-pearl; the right hand mechanism reveals a crowned shield with the arms of France, the other a winged *putto* carrying an olive branch. The silk leaf embroidered and painted with a central *vignette* of a royal baby in a cradle covered with a mantle of blue and *fleur de lys*, whilst a figure of Fame blows a trumpet, flanked by *amorini* on dolphins and beneath a painted pink ribbon bearing the message *Vive le Roy, la Reine et Monseigneur le Dauphin*; the reserves painted with two vignettes and portrait busts of Marie Antoinette and Louis XVI, the whole outlined with gold thread and coloured sequins.
Length of guard 28 cm
French c. 1781

'It was customary for the Dauphin to receive presents from the various Paris Guilds, and the celebrations to mark the birth of Louis XVI's heir, in October 1781 were particularly important. The delegations dressed in brightly coloured costumes and carrying symbols of their craft paraded in front of the royal family in the Cour Royale at Versailles…the chairmen carrying a superb gift chair on which were seated dummies representing Louis Joseph and his nurse…the gifts including pairs of babies' shoes from the shoemakers and a miniature replica of the uniform of the Dauphin's future regiment from the tailors. The locksmiths, knowing the King's skill in their craft, presented him with an ingenious trick lock. When Louis XVI opened it a tiny steel figure representing the Dauphin sprang out…'. Extracts from Barbara Scott, 'Princes' Playthings', *Country Life*, 21 June 1984.
Could this fan have been the gift of the Fan Makers?
Hélène Alexander Collection 595

## 32. *Piazza San Marco*

Ivory fan, the sticks and guards carved, pierced, painted, lacquered and gilt with figures from the *Commedia dell'Arte*. The double leaf is painted on the obverse with a view of the Piazza San Marco in Venice in the manner of Canaletto. In the reserves on the right is depicted a group of performing acrobats, on the left a peripatetic theatre. The reverse is painted with an evening view of the Venetian lagoon.

Length 30 cm
Italian c. 1750–60

Provenance: Robert Walker, Uffington, Berkshire, his sale, Sotheby, Wilkinson and Hodge, 10 June 1882. *Mr. Walker's Cabinet*, ill. pl. 52, bought Baroness Burdett Coutts; by descent to W. Burdett Coutts by 1910; Seabury Coutts, from whom purchased in 1945 by Henry S. Eeles.
The acrobats are taken from existing drawings, the background is known in many painted versions. An etching by G.B. Brustolon (*Feste Dongali* pl. 1) is the obvious source.
Lit: G. Wooliscroft Rhead, *History of the Fan*, London 1910, illus. in colour opp. p. 125.
Hélène Alexander Collection 1300

### 33. *Poem in a Landscape*

Wooden folding fan, the guards with a marquetry of bamboo. The double leaf is decorated on two different types of gold flecked paper. On the obverse the gold sprinkled paper is painted with a landscape, rustic retreats nestling among mountains. Signed T'IEH-SHENG HSI KANG with the two seals of the painter: MENG-CH'UAN and HSI KANG*. The reverse is brushed with a poem in hsing-shu written by the noted calligrapher LIANGT'UNG-SHU.
Length 30.5 cm
Chinese, Ch'ing dynasty, Hangchou, late 18th century.
*HSI KANG (1746–1803) was a well known poet and calligrapher. His landscape painting style was so unconventional technically that he was considered to have founded his own school (Paul L. Moss).
Hélène Alexander Collection 1610

The Poem on the obverse may be translated as

The endless mountains are far, far, the sun sets further still.
I have been travelling for quite some time, my empty boat vanishing into the blue mist.
Broken vines hang from the cliff,
the temple is ancient under its strange pines-
I come upon a sheer waterfall, the gentle breeze its natural echo.
The water's light, and the tone of the sky-they are like sashes, above and below,
Cluster of white colour and brightness, floating in a void.
Day and night I am homesick amid the amorphous greyness of these mountains and rivers

Reverse

Obverse

34. Pien-Mien

A fixed fan. The handle is of black lacquered wood, the frame is circular with a gold silk leaf bound with a patterned silk ribbon. The obverse is painted with peonies and insects, the reverse is decorated with a design of flowers and insects made entirely from kingfisher feathers neatly stuck over a metal backing.
Total length 42 cm
Made in China mid 19th century
Hélène Alexander Collection 600

62

## 35. The Empress of China

Large ivory cockade fan with 62 finely carved, pierced and pared sticks and elegant, elaborate deeply carved handles in an original Chinese frame of a later date. A note appended to the frame states that this fan was first purchased by a British soldier after the expedition to China in 1868. It is alleged to have come from the Summer Palace of the Empress of China and to have belonged to the French Empress Eugénie.
Length 54 cm
China c. 1800
Possibly from the Hoaching Studio.
Lit: C.L. Crossman, *The China Trade,* 1972, p. 210.
Hélène Alexander Collection

## 36. A Garland of Roses

Cockade fan of fine blond horn which is delicately pierced. Opening to a full circle, painted roses on each stick form a garland within the central parameter (on both sides). A cut steel sequin secures the rivet.
Length 17 cm (including handle)
Diameter 19.5 cm
French or Swiss c. 1808
Hélène Alexander Collection 97

### 37. *Retrato Encantador*

Mother-of-pearl fan, the sticks gilt, the guard sticks with an overlay of ormoulu wrought with a jester and a chinaman. Red paste rivet. The double paper leaf has a hand coloured etching of a dreamy young woman with four *putti* who carry a portrait of her lover. The portrait is on a movable slide concealing a mirror into which the person holding the fan beholds themselves. Inscribed *Retrato encantador, retrato de lo que adoro* (the enchanted portrait, the portrait of the one I love), i.e. when seen in the mirror! This articulated fan is the more rare as the 'articulation' is in the leaf whereas it is more usual to find the guards concealing an articulated automation.

Length 22 cm
Franco-Spanish c. 1828
Hélène Alexander Collection 1113

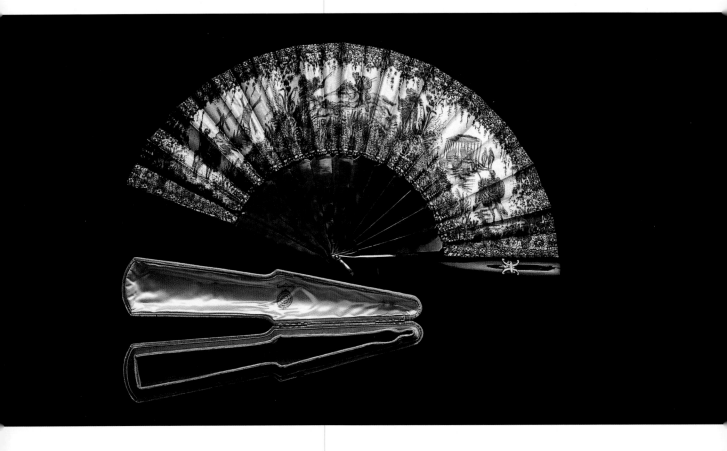

### 38. Don Quixote in Lace

Tortoiseshell fan with plain polished sticks and guards applied with the letter H entwined by a ribbon inscribed *Fanny*. The gold loop also bears the name Fanny. The black Chantilly silk lace backed with white silk shows three scenes from the story of *Don Quixote* within an elegant border of flowers. The fan comes in its own fitted blue velvet case, the lid stamped *London and Ryder, International Exhibition 1862, 17 New Bond Street – Corner of Clifford St – W.* PRIZE MEDAL.
Length 30 cm
French (possibly mounted or embellished in England) c. 1860's
Hélène Alexander Collection 189

## 39. Awakening Love

Ivory folding fan, the sticks pierced and gilt, the guards set with gilt metal plaques with turquoise and split pearls signed WEISE*. The *canepin* leaf is painted with a lady resting on a fallen column surrounded by *putti* and watched by her lover from behind a nearby tree, signed A. SOLDE*. With its own buttoned box.
Length 29cm
French c. 1865

*WEISE: Parisian jeweller, exhibited in the 1862 Exhibition.
*SOLDE, Alexandre (1822–1893). French genre painter exhibited at the Salons 1844–1868. Painted a number of known fans, including one sold at the Alexander sale of 1875. Pupil of Léon Gogniet.
Hélène Alexander Collection 425

## 40. Cherubs for a Queen

Mother-of-pearl fan, the sticks and guards carved in high relief, pierced and gilt, the guardsticks with *putti* ascending a maypole on the right guard which is inscribed *Fidelité*, at the top of which stands a *putto* with a pitcher and cup for wine. The left guard (reverse) has *putti* descending in a somewhat inebriated state. The double *canepin* leaf is painted with eight *putti* with coloured drapes bearing a garland of polychrome flowers against a blue sky, signed E. PARMENTIER*. The reverse with a crown and four minute gold bees is signed ALEXANDRE*. Fine gilt loop.
Said to have been made for Queen Isabella II of Spain.
Length 29 cm
French c. 1860–70

*PARMENTIER, E. probably Eugénie, Mme Parmentier née Morin (d.1875). She figures in the Paris Salons 1859 to 1867 with miniatures and portraits and obtained a medal in 1864. She studied with her father Gustave Morin in Rouen.
*ALEXANDRE. Fan-maker to the Empress Eugénie of France and the top nobility of Europe and Russia. See also under no. 41.
Hélène Alexander Collection 770

## 41. A Gift of Love

Mother-of-pearl folding fan, backed with *goldfish*, the sticks elaborately carved in an all over pattern of fruit and flowers enhanced with gold leaf details. The guards are encased in gold with a design of ribbons and sprays of flowers, inset with diamonds, emeralds, circular and *cabochon* cut sapphires and rubies. The gold loop is shaped to form a double love knot. There are Russian control marks on the outer edge which is also engraved with the date *4 Juin 1875*. The double paper leaf is painted on both sides. On the obverse an animated ballroom scene forms the central motif with different varieties of roses in the reserves. Signed *Aman Cy** and along the guard (on the reverse), indistinctly, *Alexandre**. The reverse is painted with three *vignettes* among a trellis and roses. In the centre the scene is a *pastiche à la Watteau*, and in the reserves the medallions feature playful *putti* with amatory devices. The rivet is set with a ruby on one side and a sapphire on the other.

Length 28.5 cm

Franco-Russian c. 1870

*AMAN (Cyboulle or Cyb), French School, painter of flowers and insects exhibited at the salon between 1868 and 1880). He was clearly popular in Russian aristocratic circles.

*ALEXANDRE, Félix. Fan maker to the French Imperial Court (he also made fans for other courts of Europe). He manufactured top quality fans between 1855 and 1875 when he liquidated his business. In 1891 a consignment of 'Alexandre' fans was brought from Paris to Russia out of which eleven were selected by the Emperor Alexander III.

Lit: *Personal Treasures of the Tsars*, catalogue p. 73; Julia Plotnikova, *Imperial Fans from the Hermitage*, catalogue p.11.

Hélène Alexander Collection 1585

## 42. The Skating Party

Ivory fan, the guardsticks carved in high relief with dolphins and masks. The ivory sticks are minutely fretted and delicately painted *en grisaille* with four vignettes of love and marriage, two of which are signed ED MOREAU*. The double *canepin* leaf is painted with a 16th-century skating scene in the centre with elegant figures in a sledge and two smaller *vignettes* showing guests arriving at a banquet with a musician, and the banquet at which the jovial host is about to be crowned by a lady in green. Signed and dated EDOUARD MOREAU 1865.
This fan is similar to one from ALEXANDRE, exhibited at Karlsruhe in 1891, (Exhibition Catalogue, pl. 26); another by Moreau, also from Alexandre, is in the Victoria and Albert Museum.
Length 30 cm
French c. 1865

*MOREAU, Edouard Jean-Baptiste (1825–1878) exhibited at the Salon between 1848 and 1878. He painted in gouache and miniatures on vellum and specialised in historic subjects.
Hélène Alexander Collection 1490

74

### 43. Antony and Cleopatra

Mother-of-pearl fan, carved and gilded. *The canepin* leaf is double, painted on the obverse in gouache with a lively scene of CLEOPATRA's* banquet. Cleopatra reclines opposite Antony; naked but for a patterned cloth knotted at the waist, she drops the pearl into her wine cup, vainly trying to capture Antony's attention, while he gazes away into the distance, garlanded and dressed in a white tunic and red mantle. On the table between them is his wine cup, a mixing bowl with a ladle and a covered goblet. Behind them dance a devotee of Isis, naked to the waist and holding a sistrum (the rattle used in the cult of Isis), and a woman wrapped in a transparent veil. A Greek lute player and an Egyptian harpist provide the music. Two men serve the royal couple, one with a fan, the other bearing a tray with a covered goblet, a small dish and a bowl of fruit. Antony and Cleopatra recline on hard couches placed on a stepped platform; in the background an awning is supported on obelisks before an Egyptian shrine set in a colonnaded garden. The pose of the figures and the architectural setting suggest an orientalized version of the principal drinking scene and the banqueting bower on a mosaic from Palestrina. The leaf is signed *J.L. VIGER**. The date of the fan coincides well with the opening in 1869 of the Suez Canal, engineered by Ferdinand de Lesseps. The *gorge* of the fan is delicately carved with a scene of the death of Cleopatra. The asp may be glimpsed slithering over the tiled floor away from Cleopatra, who reclines, her head fallen back on a bed set on a terrace with palms beyond, with her attendants Charmian and Iras. The furniture is partially gilded, as are the Egyptian figures on the guards, hieroglyphs and other decorative elements framing the scene.

Length 28 cm
French c. 1870

*CLEOPATRA – Cleopatra VII (69–30 BC), Queen of Egypt, the last of the PTOLOMIES.
*VIGER (du Vigneau) Jean Louis Victor
Lit: Dr S Walker, CLEOPATRA *of Egypt from History to Myth*, The British Museum Press, cat. 393.
Hélène Alexander Collection

44. *Stephanie's Fan*

Mother-of-pearl folding fan, the guards encased in solid gold which is ornamented with fine silver work and diamonds (there are over 1500 rose diamonds) featuring floral swags, a crown and the initial 'S'. The sticks which are backed with *goldfish* are beautifully carved with flowers, intricate tendrils and musical instruments. Gold, silver and diamond loop and two one carat yellow diamonds in the rivet. The double vellum leaf is signed and dated on both sides CESARE DELL'ACQUA* 1881. On the obverse is an important scene of figures in seventeenth century costume, on the reverse is a marriage scene in eighteenth century dress (see below for full description). The fan was a gift to STEPHANIE OF BELGIUM* for her wedding in 1881, from her uncle and aunt, the Count and Countess of Flanders.

Length 31 cm
Flemish c. 1881

*DELL'ACQUA, CESARE Félix George (1821–1904) born at Pirano (near Trieste). Studied at the Venice Accademia, specialised in historical painting and portraits. He then worked in Paris and Brussels. He achieved success with historical paintings which were exhibited in Antwerp, Brussels, Ghent, Liège, Paris and Rotterdam. The Emperor Maximilian commissioned him to paint an important series at the Palace of Miramare (1858–1866). He was also a distinguished watercolour artist.
*STEPHANIE OF BELGIUM (1864–1945), daughter of Leopold (1835–1909) and Queen Marie-Henriette (1836–1902), married Crown Prince Rudolph (Archduke Rudolf) von Hapsburg (1858–1889) in 1881. In 1900 after a long widowhood, she remarried to a Hungarian, Count Elmer of Longay de Nagy-Lonya and Vasaras-Nameny.

Description of the Painting

Obverse: an imaginary scene set against the background of a Gothic tower of the Hôtel de Ville in Brussels. In the centre stands Isabella Clara Eugenia of Hapsburg (1566–1633) receiving a fan from her court painter Peter Paul Rubens (1577–1640) while Paulus van Vianen of Utrecht (the most notable goldsmith and jeweller in the Netherlands in the early 17th century) offers gold and silver plate. Other personages are also represented in this imaginary episode in which Isabella's features are those of Stephanie and all other personages are likewise portrayed.

Reverse: the young couple (Stephanie and Rudolph) are represented in 18th century attire and are greeted by two groups converging on either side. The scene unfurls against a backdrop of landmarks such as the Imperial Bridge, St. Stephen's Cathedral, the Upper Belvedere Palace and the church of St. Charles. Two garlanded maypoles bear the couple's crowned shields, the lion of

Brabant and the Austrian double eagle. There are other relevant figures.

cf. Hélène Alexander, 'The Tale of Stephanie's Fan', *Fans* (Bulletin of the Fan Circle International) Summer 1998, issue 67, pp.38–42.

Hélène Alexander Collection 1450

### 45. Carmen Sylva

14 sticks carved and gilt with a spray of flowers, the guards applied with gold panels
enamelled in subtle pinks with yellow and green lilies, daisies and roses in Art Nouveau
style by Paul Telge, Berlin. The *canepin* leaf painted with fronds of nasturtiums signed
*Emma Fanty Lescure*.
Length of guard 32.5 cm
c.1895
In a box from Paul Telge, with appended note: 'Fan ornamented in gold enamels
designed by CARMEN SYLVA*, H.M. the Queen of Rumania'.

*CARMEN SYLVA was the pseudonym of Queen Elizabeth of Roumania who was known for
her poetry, fairy tales and novels. A somewhat eccentric lady who used to stand on the
terrace of her house at Constanza watching the sea and shouting her blessings through a
megaphone to departing ships.
Lit: N. Armstrong, *The Book of Fans*, Surrey 1978, pp. 86-7 illus.
Hélène Alexander Collection 141

### 46. *Fabergé*

Blond tortoiseshell fan, one guard applied with two-coloured goldwork, including a white *guilloché* enamel medallion with cyrillic initials, *AB* in diamonds, the medallion surrounded by rose diamonds and further delicate bows and other motifs in diamonds. The gold loop has the signature of Fabergé workmaster MICHAEL PERCHIN, St. Petersburg. The leaf is of fine *point de gaze* lace, with two good quality diamonds in the rivet.
Length 32 cm
c. 1890's

Fans such as this one were usually made in France. Often the lace came from Belgium. The additional ornament was then added in the country for which the fan was destined, by a fashionable jeweller, usually of the Court.
Hélène Alexander Collection 1177

## 47. Jewelled Night

Tortoiseshell folding fan, the sticks shaped to simulate rays of light ending in motifs forming a garland of flowers carried by *putti*. One guard stick is plain natural tortoiseshell, while the other is magnificently carved with a draped woman crowned with a diamond star set in silver with rose diamonds. Stars with rose diamonds are strewn over the whole *monture*. The double *canepin* leaf is painted on the obverse only with a pretty woman surrounded by five *putti*. She is waving dark drapery and appears to sit amidst dark blue clouds upon which are studded stars of rose diamond and rock crystal. The rivet is capped by a jewelled star of silver with rose diamonds.
Signed G. LASELLAZ*'92
Length 35.5 cm
French c. 1892

*LASELLAZ, Gustave-François, b. Paris, belonged to the Société Des Artistes Français; he exhibited at this salon from 1883. He painted many fans for Maison Duvelleroy.
Hélène Alexander Collection 1422

## 48. *Sea 'Breezes'*

Ivory and mother-of-pearl *fontange* fan. The sticks and guards are of sculptured mother-of-pearl with marine motifs applied, including delicately carved mermaids. The double leaf is painted on both sides, the obverse with marine nymphs and mermaids enjoying the delights of the sea. The nymphs sail in shells drawn by seagulls, their hair crowned with coral or seashells. The reverse depicts a quieter seascape with a classical vessel, a beach and one frightened seagull.

Signed on the obverse MAURICE LELOIR*. The reverse is quite clearly also by the same hand.

Overall length 29 cm

French c.1900

*LELOIR, Maurice (1851–1938). Founded the French Costume Society – went to America for a time to design for early Hollywood films such as *The Three Musketeers*.

Hélène Alexander Collection 1452

*49. 'Brambles'*

Horn *brisé* fan carved with brambles and foliage and backed with mother-of-pearl and abalone and groups of black berries applied in dark mother-of-pearl. Amber rivet.
Signed G. BASTARD*
Length 18.5 cm
French c. 1908

*BASTARD: *tabletier* (fan-stick-maker), mentioned in the *Almanach du Commerce* for the Oise (France) in 1900, working in Andeville.
Lit: *L'Éventail Miroir de la Belle Epoque*, cat. no. 62, plate 14, p.29.
Hélène Alexander Collection 1455

50. *Bird of Paradise*

Mother-of-pearl and feather fan, the entire
bird of paradise feathers are reconstituted
into a fan, complete with stuffed head: the
very best of the French feather trade!
Tooled metal loop.
Overall length approx. 40 cm
French c. 1918
Hélène Alexander Collection 1582

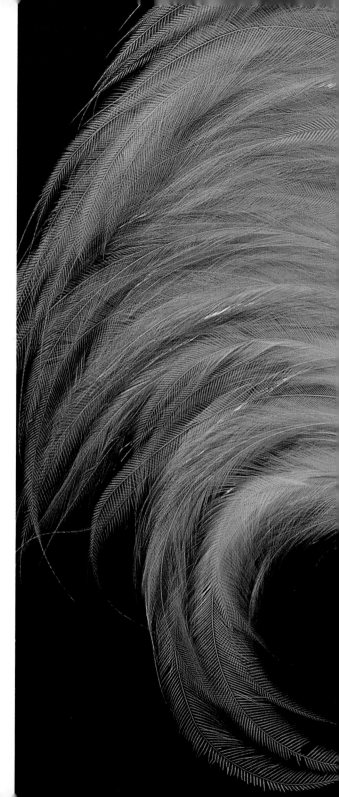

**A l'anglaise:** A technique regularly used throughout the centuries where the ribs are applied to a single leaf and are therefore visible on the reverse of the fan. Sometimes the ribs are emphasised with a coloured line, other times they are painted over.

**Appliqué:** Applied – either sewn or stuck on.

**Brisé:** A folding fan consisting of sticks only, forming a flat surface when open, held together at the top by a cord or ribbon, threaded, slotted or stuck on; i.e. a fan with no leaf.

**Canepin:** Fine kid or imitation kid, used for fan leaves.

**Chicken skin:** Very fine kid, which resembles paper.

**Chinoiserie:** A term adopted to describe the European fashion for articles in the Chinese taste. At its height from the late 17th century to the end of the 18th century.

**Cloisonné:** A form of enamel work on metal mesh or filigree, usually made in the Orient, in which the designs are supported by vertical partitions which help to retain the vitreous substance.

**Clouté:** Applied or inset plaques of mother-of-pearl or other substances pinned with metal thread (usually gold or silver).

**Contrepanache:** Literally: against the guard. A contrepanache is a third guardstick, usually applied to the left guardstick so that, when the fan is open, the leaf on the obverse is framed by two guards, thus giving a more symmetrical aspect to the leaf.

**Cockade:** Fans which can be brisé or pleated opening up around the pivot set at the centre of the fan (as opposed to being at its base). The fan therefore is circular or semi-circular in shape and is sometimes called parasol or circular fan.

**Etched:** Engraved by the etching method.

**Éventail:** Fan (French).

**Filigree:** Ornamental work of gold, silver or copper wire formed into delicate tracery.

**Folding fan:** A fan which closes up on itself.

**Fontange:** Name given to the type of fan in which the guardsticks are shorter than the leaf at its apex, producing a fan of elongated and rounded appearance – sometimes referred to as arched. (Forme ballon and palmette are variants).

**Forme Ballon:** See Fontange.

**Goldfish:** A very fine translucent mother-of-pearl often used to back carved white mother-of-pearl.

**Gorge:** The part of the fan immediately above the pivot end, and beneath the leaf.

**Gouache:** Opaque water colour paint thickened with gum and honey; pictures thus painted.

**Guards:** The two outer sticks of a fan, usually stouter and more highly decorated.

**Handle:** See Monture.

**Hand screen:** A rigid fan, shaped, usually square or circular, mounted on a handle.

**Kid:** Soft leather (from a baby goat or chamois).

**Lacquer:** Varnish used as a coating (over paint).

**Leaf:** See 'Mount'.

**Loop:** A curved attachment to the head of the fan, held in place by the rivet, whereby a fan may be suspended from a cord, ribbon or chatelaine.

**Monture:** The part of the fan upon which the leaf is mounted, comprising the sticks, guards and rivet; i.e. the skeleton.

**Monture:** With a monture sultane the ribs of the fan, usually ornamental, à la Sultane are visible on the obverse of the fan. Demi-sultane is when only a few and demi-of the ribs show on the leaf.

**Motif:** A repeated theme in a design, or distinctive features.

**Mount or leaf:** The portion of the fan which is placed onto and over the ribs. It can be pleated and made from a variety of materials. It may be single or double.

**Obverse:** The front of the fan. The public face of the fan; the side facing the viewer.

**Parchment:** An animal skin, the surface of which is prepared for writing or painting.

**Pavé:** (jewellery term) Tiny sequins or other small surfaces superimposed or placed so close together as to form an even, flat-looking surface.

**Picot:** A lace-like edging.

**Piqué:** A form of decoration mainly on tortoiseshell and ivory, developed in Italy, consisting of decorative shapes made by dots of precious metal (gold or silver) set into the host material.

**Pivot:** A small rod inserted through the lower part of the sticks (the head) of the fan and around which the fan can revolve. It is terminated at either end by a stop which holds it in place and prevents slipping. These stops are sometimes referred to as pivot ends or rivets, and sometimes made of paste, mother-of-pearl etc, etc. In special cases they can be small jewelled buttons.

**Pongé** de soie  A silk gauze fabric slightly elasticated.

**Putti:** Plural of putto (a small cherub without wings).

**Reserves:** The spaces in the outer part of the fan leaf containing a decoration subordinate to the main picture.

**Ribs:** The upper part of the sticks which support the leaf.

**Rivet:** See Pivot.

**Rocaille:** Decorative style characterised by fantasies of rounded lines and shell shapes which flourished in France in the reign of Louis XV.

**Rococo:** A style of decoration common in 18th-century Europe, typified by asymmetrical patterns involving scroll work and shell motifs.

**Shoulder:** That part of the stick/guard where leaf and gorge meet.

**Skin:** The term used to designate a leaf made from an animal source without attempting to identify the specific species.

**Spangles:** Pressed metal shapes.

**Sticks:** The principal part of the fan, the skeleton as it were, which also contains the articulation.

**Vernis Martin:** A varnish invented by the Martin family (c.1720–1758). 'Vernis Martin' fans are usually of the brisé kind and so called because their painted, varnished surface appears to resemble known work from the Martin workshop.

**Vignette:** Small illustration, not usually the primary pictorial design.

**Washer** Small (usually) circular stop, which can be mother-of-pearl or other material, placed over the rivet at either side of the fan to prevent it from slipping.

| | Name of Exhibition | Period of Exhibition | |
|---|---|---|---|
| 1 | Children in Fans | 5 May 1991 | 24 September 1991 |
| 2 | Fans of the Four Seasons | 26 September 1991 | 15 January 1992 |
| 3 | Homage to the Donor | 17 January 1992 | 7 June 1992 |
| 4 | Fine Feathers make Fine Fans | 9 June 1992 | 1 October 1992 |
| 5 | Hatch, Match and Despatch | 13 October 1992 | 21 March 1993 |
| 6 | Flowers and Fans | 23 March 1993 | 3 October 1993 |
| 7 | Fans and the China Trade | 5 October 1993 | 20 March 1994 |
| 8 | A Flutter of Lace | 22 March 1994 | 17 July 1994 |
| 9 | Fans on the Grand Tour | 19 July 1994 | 22 January 1995 |
| 10 | Unfolding Beauty:– A Secret Collection | 24 January 1995 | 14 May 1995 |
| 11 | Collector's Choice | 16 May 1995 | 1 October 1995 |
| 12 | Duvelleroy – King of Fans, fan-maker to Kings | 3 October 1995 | 21 January 1996 |
| 13 | Animal Fans | 23 January 1996 | 2 June 1996 |
| 14 | Now & Then | 4 June 1996 | 3 November 1996 |
| 15 | Theatrical Fans | 5 November 1996 | 9 March 1997 |
| 16 | Adam & Eve and Fans | 11 March 1997 | 29 June 1997 |
| 17 | Fans from Far Away Lands | 1 July 1997 | 10 October 1997 |
| 18 | Imperial Fans from The Hermitage | 17 October 1997 | February 1998 |
| 19 | Poetry on the Breeze | 23 February 1998 | 7 June 1998 |
| 20 | Flowers that Bloom on the Fans (TraLa) | 9 June 1998 | 8 November 1998 |
| 21 | Personal Treasures of the Tsars | 20 November 1998 | 20 March 1999 |
| 22 | Advertising Fans | 28 March 1999 | 25 July 1999 |
| 23 | Match the Fan | 27 July 1999 | 19 December 1999 |
| 24 | Commemorative Fans | 21 December 1999 | 23 April 2000 |
| 25 | Sea Breezes | 25 April 2000 | 27 August 2000 |
| 26 | The Jewel and the Fan | 29 August 2000 | 3 December 2000 |
| 27 | Art Nouveau | 9 December 2000 | 4 March 2001 |
| 28 | From the Land of the Fan | 7 March 2001 | 24 June 2001 |
| 29 | Masterpieces of The Fan Museum | 26 June 2001 | 27 November 2001 |